This edition published in 1999 by Blitz Editions
an imprint of Bookmart Limited
Registered Number 2372865
trading as Bookmart Limited
Desford Road
Enderby
Leicester
LE9 5AD

Published and produced by ADC International - 1998 Eke Nazareth - Belgium
Printed in Dubai, 1999

Three Little Pigs

'''VAN GOOL'''

Mother and Father Pig lived happily on their country farm with their three little sons. There was always much work to be done, but there were many hands to help, and the pig family raised all the food they needed. One morning, while Father hoed the garden and Mother fed the chickens, the three little pigs decided they were grown up enough to leave home to seek their fortunes.

"There's a big, beautiful world out there," exclaimed the middle pig, pointing to the door.

"I'm going to be rich," mused the youngest pig, chewing on a piece of straw.

"Stop dreaming and finish packing!" said the oldest pig. "We must get going soon."

As the three little pigs prepared to leave, their parents offered advice. "Always stay together," said Mother Pig, "and be careful with your money."

"Beware of the wolf!" added Father Pig sternly. "He is fierce and clever, and likes nothing better than pig for breakfast."

The oldest pig listened carefully. "Don't worry," he said. "We'll be fine. When we're settled you can come to visit."

The younger pigs danced and giggled, chattering about their grand adventure.

"Hurry up, lazybones!" exclaimed the youngest pig, setting off with his brother.

"Bye, Mother!" called the pigs.

"Don't forget to brush your teeth!" Mother called back. "And send a postcard!"

As the three little pigs disappeared over the hill, Mother Pig dabbed at her tears. "I'll miss them so!" she cried.

Father Pig gave her a hug. "They'll be okay," he said. "They'll help each other."

The three little pigs walked a long way. They ate the picnic lunch their mother had packed. "Let's have a nap," said the youngest pig. "I can't walk another step."

"Ah, this is the life!" sighed the middle pig.

"We have to keep going," replied the oldest. "We have to find the best spot to build our house."

The pigs made slow progress. When they passed through a village the younger brothers stopped to buy sweets and play games. The oldest pig urged them along. When they emerged from a forest the youngest pig exclaimed, “Look! The perfect place for our house!”

“Oh, no!” protested the oldest. “This is too close to the forest, where the wolf may live.”

The younger pigs burst into laughter. "Who's afraid of the big, bad wolf?" they sang, taunting their brother.

"Don't be such a sissy!" said the middle pig. "We've walked all day, and haven't seen any sign of the wolf!"

"This is not a good place to settle," insisted the oldest pig. "The wolf likes the woods."

"Well, we're not leaving!" said the youngest pig.

"Then I'll go and build my own house in a sensible place!" shouted the oldest pig, storming away.

A short while later the oldest pig returned to his brothers. “I’m going into town to buy bricks and cement to build my house,” he said. “If you come along you can do the same.”

“But we have no money!” wailed the youngest pig.

“We spent it on sweets and games,” added the middle pig. “Besides, it’s too much work to build a brick house.”

So the oldest pig trotted off to town by himself, and returned with a wheelbarrow filled with all the things he needed. “I can’t leave my little brothers by themselves near the forest,” he said to himself. “I’ll build my house nearby so I can look after them.”

The oldest pig set to work staking out his plot and sketching his house design. His brothers gathered sticks and straw for their houses.

"Bad idea!" exclaimed the oldest pig. "Your houses won't be strong enough to keep out the wolf."

But the little pigs only laughed. "We're not afraid of the wolf!" replied the youngest.

The pigs all set to work on their houses. Soon the two younger pigs had finished making their houses, one of straw and one of sticks. They found their older brother, still busy building his brick house.

“You’re crazy to work so hard!” shouted the youngest pig, laughing.

“Go ahead and laugh,” replied the oldest pig. “We’ll see who the crazy ones are when the wolf comes!”

“So long!” called the middle pig gleefully. “We’re going for a walk.”

The two little pigs sauntered along. They picked flowers and berries, watched birds, played hide-and-seek, and even found a secret cave in the woods. But with night approaching the little pigs returned to their houses. They didn't know that the wolf watched them from the woods, and cautiously followed to see where they went.

It was dark by the time the oldest pig climbed down from the roof. He walked around the house, admiring his beautiful work. Satisfied, he went inside and locked the door.

Soon a full moon rose over the treetops, and the wolf howled into the night. His wild howls could be heard all over the countryside.

In his brick house, the oldest pig shivered. “It’s the wolf!” he whispered. “He knows we’re here. I hope my brothers are safe.” The pig sang to himself as he made dinner, so he wouldn’t hear the wolf.

In the morning the oldest pig invited his brothers to breakfast. "I'm glad you are okay," said the oldest pig. "Last night I heard the wolf howling."

The youngest pig jumped down from the table, frightened.

"Now look what you've done with your crazy talk of wolves!" cried the middle pig. "You've scared Shorty."

The two young pigs left in a huff.

The youngest pig went home to his straw house. He had scarcely shut the door when he heard running footsteps, then a loud *knock! knock!* on the door.

"Little pig, little pig, let me come in!" came a wolfish voice.

“Not by the hair on my chinny chin chin,” replied the frightened little pig.

The wolf replied, “Then I’ll huff, and I’ll puff, and I’ll blow your house down!”

"Go away!" cried the pig.

"You think you can keep me out with this flimsy little house?" demanded the wolf. Then he drew in a tremendous breath, and blew with all his might. The straw house blew apart.

But by the time the straw floated to the ground, the little pig had dashed across the stream to his brother's stick house.

"Aha!" said the wolf, smiling. "Two little pigs for breakfast!" And he trotted to the stick house and knocked on the door. "Little pig, little pig, let me come in!" called the wolf.

"Not by the hair on my chinny chin chin," replied the middle pig.

"Then I'll huff, and I'll puff, and I'll…

… blow your house down!" snarled the wolf.

While the little pigs huddled inside, the wolf huffed and puffed, and blew and blew. It was stronger than the straw house, but before long the wolf had also blown the stick house into bits.

But the little pigs had climbed out of the window at the back, and ran as fast as their little legs could carry them. By the time the wolf blew down the house, they were gone.

The hungry wolf searched through the sticks, furious that his breakfast had escaped again. Then he saw the little pigs running to their brother's brick house. "Oh no, you don't!" snarled the wolf, dashing after them.

The oldest pig heard cries for help, and opened his door just in time for his brothers to dash in. The wolf was close behind. The pig slammed the door and locked it tight.

"Don't worry," he said to his frightened brothers. "I'm a lot smarter than that old wolf!"

The wolf stopped outside the door. "It's my lucky day," he thought smugly. "Three little pigs for breakfast!" Then he knocked on the door, and shouted, "Little pig, little pig, let me come in!"

"Not by the hair on my chinny chin chin!" answered three voices.

"Then I'll huff, and I'll puff, and I'll blow your house down!" cried the wolf.

The two young pigs huddled on the floor. But the oldest pig was busy bracing the windows and doors with planks and nails.

The wolf huffed, and puffed, and blew and blew until he was out of breath, but the brick house stood strong. Then there was silence.

The wolf had found a ladder around the back, and tiptoed around the house to the chimney side.

The oldest pig peeked out the window, and saw the wolf's plan at once.

"What'll we do?" cried the youngest pig.

The wolf began to climb the ladder up to the roof.

"Quick!" called the oldest pig, lighting a fire in the fireplace. "Fill the pot with water."

The pigs set the pot into the fireplace, where a blazing fire hissed and crackled. The water was heating to a boil when the wolf's husky voice boomed down the chimney: "I'm here, and now you can't escape!"

The wolf began to lower himself down the chimney, holding onto the bricks. He chuckled at his own cleverness.

Suddenly a brick broke off in his paws, and the wolf went plunging down the chimney. He landed with a tremendous, hissing splash in the pot of boiling water.

“Yow!” howled the wolf. “Ow! Ow! Ow!” He jumped off the pot. The oldest pig had opened the door, and the wolf raced out, clutching his scalded rear. Now it was the pigs’ turn to laugh as the wolf raced away over the hillside, never to be seen again.

“We did it!” cheered the pigs. The two younger pigs jumped up and down and hugged their big brother.

"You saved us all!" cried the middle pig.
"You were brilliant!" exclaimed the youngest pig.
"That old wolf will never bother us again," said the oldest pig with a smile, "as long as we stick together."